Honeyguide Birds and Ratels

By Kevin Cunningham

21st Century
Junior Library

Published in the United States of America by
Cherry Lake Publishing
Ann Arbor, Michigan
www.cherrylakepublishing.com

Content Adviser: Stephen Ditchkoff, Professor of Wildlife Ecology and Management, Auburn University, Alabama
Reading Adviser: Marla Conn MS, Ed., Literacy specialist, Read-Ability, Inc.

Photo Credits: © Ewan Chesse/Shutterstock, cover, 1, 10; © Sainam51/Shutterstock, 4; © Sebastian Kennerknecht/ Minden Pictures/Newscom, 6; © Lukyslukys | Dreamstime.com - Honey Badger Photo, 8; © Erwin Niemand/Shutterstock, 12; © gisela gerson lohman-braun/Flickr, 14; © imageBROKER / Alamy Stock Photo, 16; © Fotolotti | Dreamstime.com - Swarm Of Bees Photo, 18; © FLPA / Alamy Stock Photo, 20

Library of Congress Cataloging-in-Publication Data

Names: Cunningham, Kevin, 1966- author.
Title: Honeyguide birds and Ratels / Kevin Cunningham.
Description: Ann Arbor, MI : Cherry Lake Publishing, [2016] | Series: Better together |
  Audience: K to grade 3. | Includes bibliographical references and index.
Identifiers: LCCN 2015049540| ISBN 9781634710862 (hardcover) | ISBN 9781634712842 (pbk.) |
  ISBN 9781634711852 (pdf) | ISBN 9781634713832 (ebook)
Subjects: LCSH: Mutualism (Biology)—Juvenile literature. | Honeyguides—Juvenile literature. |
  Honey badger—Juvenile literature. | Animal behavior—Juvenile literature.
Classification: LCC QH548.3 .C864 2016 | DDC 591.7/85—dc23
LC record available at http://lccn.loc.gov/2015049540

Cherry Lake Publishing would like to acknowledge the work of The Partnership for 21st Century Skills.
Please visit *www.p21.org* for more information.

Printed in the United States of America
Corporate Graphics

CONTENTS

A honeyguide bird is also known as an indicator bird or a honey bird.

Over Here

The honeyguide flies from tree to tree.
It gives a **call** when it lands. The bird waits.
Then it takes off. It lands on another tree
and calls again.

A ratel, or honey badger, follows the bird
from the ground. A ratel moves fast on its
short legs. It catches up quickly.

Ratels and honeyguide birds share the same habitat.

The honeyguide and ratel want to eat. Where's the food? In a nearby beehive. The honeyguide and ratel work together to find a meal. Their amazing **relationship** helps each animal survive.

Ratels live in Africa and parts of Asia, such as India.

Rough and Tough

The ratel isn't the biggest animal around. The largest ones only reach about 9 inches (23 centimeters) tall. They weigh between 12 and 32 pounds (5.4 to 14.5 kilograms).

Ask Questions!

Some animals have false names. A honey badger isn't a badger at all, though its relatives include badgers, as well as weasels and skunks. Ask a parent, teacher, or librarian how the ratel got its other name. Find out about other animals with false names.

A ratel has very tough skin. This makes it difficult for predators to wound a ratel.

But few animals will tangle with a ratel. They have terrible tempers. Their sharp claws make them dangerous. A ratel also has a special **gland** near its bottom. The gland lets out an awful smell.

Ratels seem to have superpowers. Something in their blood makes them **immune** to snake poison.

Even a fierce hunter like a leopard must be careful. Ratels twist their bodies to bite and scratch.

The ratel is an **omnivore**. It eats many kinds of meat, eggs, and fruits. It even

The long claws on a ratel's front feet are for digging and fighting.

hunts deadly snakes like cobras. Its strong jaws can crack a tortoise's shell.

But the hardworking honeyguide helps the ratel find a very different favorite food.

Create!

Pretend that people eat bugs. Draw pretend packages of insect snacks for people to buy at the store. The food can be cereal, macaroni and cheese, gummy candy, or anything else. Make the packages funny or gross!

There are 17 species of honeyguide birds in the world.

Bird Helper

Several **species** of honeyguides live in Africa. The greater honeyguide, the largest species, can grow to 7 inches (17.8 cm) long. Honeyguides often eat insects.

The honeyguide plays a part in **folktales** in Africa. One folktale in the Ila language tells why the birds point out beehives.

A honeyguide has a special call it uses when it finds honey.

In the story, a character named Honey-guide found a wife in Bee-town. Later, though, the bees took the wife away. Honey-guide was angry. From that day on, Honey-guide led creatures to the bees' hives.

Those creatures include humans. Honeyguides have led people to honey for ages.

Think!

Folktales include nursery rhymes. Can you remember any nursery rhymes with animal characters? What do the animals do in the rhymes?

Bees live and make honey all over the world. The only places bees do not live are places where it's cold all year round.

Sweet Honey

Have a grown-up shake a box of matches. That's close to the sound made by a honeyguide when it finds a beehive.

A ratel notices the bird's call. It follows the honeyguide.

Both animals reach the tree. The ratel climbs. It tears open the beehive with its claws. The angry bees **swarm** to scare it away, but its thick skin makes it immune to bee stings.

One of the only species in the world that eats beeswax
as part of its diet is the honeyguide.

Ratels love to eat insects. Inside the beehive are thousands of insect **larvae** and adult bees. It's a **feast**! The ratel also slurps up any honey the bees have made.

The honeyguide eats all of these foods, too. It also eats the wax that bees use to build their hives. But the honeyguide is unable to open the hive on its own.

The honeyguide does part of the work. The ratel does part of the work. Their teamwork means both get to enjoy a delicious feast.

GLOSSARY

call (KAWL) a sound made by a bird, and other types of animals

feast (FEEST) a big meal

folktales (FOHK-taylz) old stories told through speaking instead of writing

gland (GLAND) a part of the body that gives off a special liquid

immune (ih-MYOON) not affected by something

larvae (LAHR-vee) baby insects

omnivore (AHM-nuh-vor) an animal that eats both meat and plants

relationship (ri-LAY-shuhn-ship) the way in which two or more things are connected

species (SPEE-sheez) one of the groups into which animals and plants of the same genus are divided

swarm (SWORM) to move together in a large group as bees do

FIND OUT MORE

BOOKS

Bates, Matthew. *Inside Beehives*. New York: PowerKids, 2015.

Gates, Margo. *Honey Badgers*. Minneapolis: Bellwether, 2013.

Jenkins, Steve, with Robin Page. *How to Clean a Hippopotamus: A Look at Unusual Animal Partnerships*. New York: HMH Books, 2010.

Machajewski, Sarah. *Life of a Honey Badger*. New York: Rosen, 2014.

Roesser, Marie. *Honey Badgers*. New York: Gareth Stevens, 2015.

WEB SITES

Discovery.com—Human Planet: Follow the Honeyguide
www.discovery.com/tv-shows/human-planet/videos/follow-the
-honeyguide-deleted

National Geographic Wild: Honey Badgers
http://channel.nationalgeographic.com/wild/galleries/honey
-badgers/at/honey-badger5-441334

PBS—Honey Badgers: Masters of Mayhem (video)
www.pbslearningmedia.org/resource/nat14.sci.lifsci.masters/honey
-badgers-masters-of-mayhem

INDEX

ABOUT THE AUTHOR

Kevin Cunningham is the author of more than 60 books. He lives near Chicago.